I0777594

NINJA
Vol. II
WARRIOR WAYS
OF ENLIGHTENMENT

Text and verses
by
Stephen K. Hayes

Edited by Bill Griffeth and Gregory Lee

Graphic Design by Karen Massad

©Ohara Publications, Incorporated 1981
All rights reserved
Printed in the United States of America
Library of Congress, Catalog Card No.: 81-83991
ISBN No.: 0-89750-077-6
Second Printing 1982

OHARA **[]** PUBLICATIONS, INCORPORATED
BURBANK, CALIFORNIA

DEDICATION

This book is dedicated to
Kikyo, Nighthawk, Dragonfly, *and* Greensnake,
better known as Rumiko, Larry, Bud and M,
the founding members of
the Shadows of Iga Original House,
for all those years of loyal support
that aided me in introducing the teachings
of authentic Japanese ninjutsu
to the western world.

Nin-po ik-kan!

ACKNOWLEDGEMENT

Without the generosity of Dr. Masaaki Hatsumi, 34th grandmaster of Togakure ryu ninjutsu, the western world would know little more of ninjutsu than a few overexaggerated legends and distorted myths. As the head master of Japan's only remaining historically-traceable ninjutsu system, Dr. Hatsumi patiently guided me along the path leading to the ninja's realm of knowledge and power. All that I have been able to bring back to the west is a direct result of Dr. Hatsumi's encouragement, openness, frankness, and willingness to share the keys to the ultimate secrets of the warrior's heart. This book and its contents are then a salute to grandmaster Masaaki Hatsumi, the teacher whose lessons and years spent in guiding me are all the more meaningful now that he no longer accepts new personal students.   S.K.H.

ABOUT THE AUTHOR

Stephen K. Hayes, America's foremost authority on the art and practice of ninjutsu, was born in Delaware, grew up in Ohio, and graduated from Miami University in Oxford, Ohio, with a BA degree in theater. The author began his commitment to the martial arts as a way of life in the mid-60s, and has spent his entire adult life in pursuit of the total development possible through the original warrior ways of the East.

Stephen K. Hayes is the first non-Oriental to ever receive the title of *shidoshi,* or "teacher of the warrior ways of enlightenment," in the centuries-old Japanese tradition of ninjutsu. He is the sole American teacher to hold the shidoshi title for the current generation. As part of the responsibility inherited with the title, the author has been granted the license to establish his own Togakure ryu ninjutsu branch training organization under the authority of Dr. Masaaki Hatsumi, the 34th grandmaster of Togakure ryu.

With the support and assistance of his students, Stephen K. Hayes founded the Shadows of Iga society of ninjutsu scholars and enthusiasts in 1975, for the purpose of disseminating the benefits of the knowledge of Japan's ninja in the western world, and for the additional purpose of bringing together those persons who felt it their destiny to become a part of the ninja tradition. Three years later, the Shadows of Iga became the supervisory organization for the direction of Togakure ryu ninjutsu training in the English-speaking world. The international society now has representative members in the United States, Canada, United Kingdom, Australia, Germany, Sweden, India, Israel and Japan.

Persons interested in joining the Shadows of Iga can write to the society at: Shadows of Iga, P.O. Box 1947, Kettering, OH 45429 USA.

CONTENTS

CHAPTER ONE

Ninjutsu skills
  in which we train
  would best be known as the art of winning.
We will assist the sincere
  with our ability to win with the spirit.
Their dreams become the force of our vision
  which becomes a vibrant intention
  taking shape in the mind
  and weaving into the fabric of reality.

SPIRITUAL PURITY
Ninja morality in history

 ttaining the core essence of the ninja art begins with the paring away of unessentials to reach a base state of personal spiritual purity, and culminates in the ability to move freely without defilement between the polar realms of brightness and darkness, as necessitated by the scheme of totality."

According to the observations of Yasuyoshi Fujibayashi, this is what it means to be a ninja. In his 17th-century encyclopedia of ninjutsu, the *Bansenshukai,* Fujibayashi has noted that the ultimate purpose of the ninja's art lies not in the mere perfection of violent and destructive methods, but in the cultivation of personal harmony with the surroundings and an intuitive sensitivity that permits the living mortal human to know and go along with the scheme of totality that flows through the universe.

Despite the emphasis on spiritual purity, the ninja art has never really been accepted by the historical Japanese martial community as one of the *do* disciplines, those zen-like practices said to be a means of attaining enlightenment. During the peaceful centuries that followed the Tokugawa family's unification of Japan, the once warlike samurai technique systems such as *kenjutsu* (sword combat), *jujutsu* (unarmed combat), *kyujutsu* (archery), *jojutsu* (staff fighting), *iaijutsu* (fast-draw sword), and others were systematized, stylized, and refined to become cultural exercises like *kendo, judo, kyudo, jodo,* and *iaido.* This ritualization of a previously personalized and spontaneous activity is fairly typical of the Japanese way of doing things. Since the ways of war were no longer required, and in fact were not encouraged at all by the Tokugawa rulers, the physical aspects of combat that were so familiar to all were simply adjusted slightly and given a new purpose for continuation.

This ritualization process had its roots in previous centuries of Japanese cultural history when the learning of the *Gokyo* Five Classics of Chinese literature was a requirement for attaining the status of a government officer in pre-Heian Japan, just as it had been in China. Though the repeated exposure to the Chinese classics had little direct relevance to the daily activities and decisions required of the ancient Japanese ruling class, it was probably felt that the learning process itself was the purpose of the study. This attitude was later carried over to the ways of *sado* (ceremonial preparation of green tea), and *kado* (recitation of poetry). Beyond this, the *do* concept came to include the *shudo* art of the written character, the *kado* art of arranging flowers, and the numerous ways of the martial tradition.

The ninja's art is conspicuously absent from the list of *do* disciplines, because the ninja existed as cultural opposites of the samurai who generated the *do* concept. The secrets of the ninja art were known by only a few families who were then referred to as *Iga-mono* and *Koga-mono,* depending on which of the two remote regions they inhabited. They were not usually given the samurai title of *bushi.* For this reason, the knowledge was not well-known to samurai society. The physical aspects of the ninja's art were pragmatic applications of the ninja's mystical understanding of the universe, and due to that very pragmatism and lack of formality, did not lend themselves well to the stylization necessary for the transformation to a *do* art.

According to the *Bansenshukai's* Iga ryu ninja Yasuyoshi Fujibayashi, as well as later authorities such as Kogu ryu ninja Seiko Fujita and

Togakure ryu ninja Shinryuken Masamitsu Toda, the art of the true ninja is much more than the mere technique system than the word *ninjutsu* would imply. Since the ninja art is not of samurai origin, thereby making *nindo* a cultural impossibility, and since the practitioner of the ninja art is expected to approach personal enlightenment *before* learning the combat techniques, the more advanced ninja of later Japanese history (following the founding of the Tokugawa Shogunate in 1603) have preferred to call their art *nin-po*, or "the law of the *shinobi* (ninja) realm."

The Bansenshukai

Fujibayashi's *Bansenshukai,* literally translated as "Ten-thousand Rivers Collect in the Sea," is a collection of knowledge and commentaries on attitude from dozens of ninja family systems that thrived in the Iga and Koga regions of South Central Japan. Historical authorities characterize the writings as extremely systematic and logical, both in the scope of knowledge contained and the thorough way in which the topics are itemized. The original work was compiled by Yasuyoshi Fujibayashi in the summer of 1676, during the reign of the fourth Tokugawa Shogun. Fujibayashi was a member of one of the three most influential Iga ninja families; the Hattori and Momochi families being the other two of the three in prominence at the close of the *sengoku jidai* warring states period.

The first of the ten hand-bound volumes contains an introduction, historical examples, an index of the contents, and a question-and-answer section. The guiding philosophy of the ninja is presented in this first volume entitled *Jo*, as a discussion of successful warfare. The ninja is admonished to remember that when a leader truly guides the minds of his followers, even great numbers of adversaries can be overcome. When a leader's or a commander's followers are not in alignment with his thoughts, failure and loss will surely result. One spy or counteracting agent can bring the downfall of an entire army. Therefore, the ninja believes that one person can defeat thousands. The *Bansenshukai* stresses that ninjutsu is the most effective method of military strategy.

The second volume is entitled *Shoshin,* and it discusses the sincerity, motivation, and moral strength of intention necessary for the ninja. Since the skills of the ninja's art admittedly include methods that some individuals would call treachery, deception, theft, and fraud—not to mention incredibly thorough violence—a strong statement of purpose and outlook is presented before going into techniques. In previous centuries, just as today, the majority of people seemed to feel that any thug, mercenary, or terrorist dressed in a black costume and hood could be called a ninja. Some may point out that the techniques and practices seem to appear similar in nature, but the true ninja is set apart by his motivation, purpose, and scope of vision. The mere terrorist or mercenary is limited by a narrow frame of reference and a restricted concept of the total picture, of which his actions, reactions, and thoughts make up an influencing part. The true ninja is prompted to act through a personal realization of responsibility recognizable only through an intuitive knowledge that destiny has demanded his taking part. The first step in the ninja's education, whether the process be called ninjutsu or nin-po, is to clear up any mental or spiritual cloudiness that would interfere with the ninja's natural sense of knowing.

Even the most skilled of ninja is useless without the guidance and direction of an effective leader. The third book, *Shochi,* covers the methods of managing a ninja organization and ways of successfully using ninja. This third volume also describes considerations for preventing enemy agents from working into the ninja leader's own clandestine organization.

A working knowledge of *in* and *yo* (*yin* and *yang* in the Chinese language) balancing is crucial for true knowledge of the ninja art. *Yo-nin,* the fourth of the ten volumes, deals with the *yo,* or bright side of the ninja's power. Using the dynamic and positive power of the intellect and creative thinking, the ninja can obtain the intelligence information he needs without becoming physically involved in the spying activity himself. By directly or indirectly employing others to gain his knowledge for him, the ninja knows all the necessary facts for an effective military decision. By learning the enemy strengths and weaknesses, the ninja knows how to handle the enemy successfully, while maintaining the appearance of having done nothing or of having taken no action.

The methods of knowing the enemy's intentions without taking active part in combat action include:

- *Tonyu hen:* for continuous observation through agents placed during peaceful times.
- *Kinnyu hen:* for location of agents after war breaks out.
- *Mekiki hen:* for observation of the geographical layout of the enemy's territory.
- *Miwake hen:* for observation of enemy force numbers and capabilities, along with other details of enemy strength.
- *Kanmi hen:* for observation of the enemy's strategy and positioning.

The fifth, sixth, and seventh volumes of the *Bansenshukai,* all titled *Innin,* deal with the *in* or dark side of the ninja's power. Using stealth, deception, confusion tactics, and terrifying surprise attacks, the ninja could bring the enemy under his control. Employing methods that the conventional samurai of the time considered to be dishonorable, contemptible, and even cowardly, the ninja were free to rely on disguises, night fighting, sneaking in, capturing enemy leaders, and cultivating key enemy personnel for betrayal in order to accomplish their aims. Volumes five, six, and seven contain these unique methods of the ninja combat system, from individual clashes to group hit-and-scatter plans.

The techniques themselves are most often presented in cryptic or poetic wordings to prevent the uninitiated from picking up the manuscript and learning the secrets. For example, in one passage the ninja is reminded of the effectiveness of *murasame no jutsu* (art of the rain in the village), in certain specific situations. The actual technique itself is not explained. Combat moves such as *onikudaki* (demon crusher) appear unexplained in their poetic form. The literal rendering of the name as "inward uplifting elbow leverage to dislocate the shoulder of the attacker" for the identical technique was apparently thought to be too direct for the written record. Such a name would not have been in keeping with the tradition of mystery that surrounded the ninja and their art, and would have made that technique all too clear to any enemy who happened to obtain a stolen copy of the *Bansenshukai.*

The methods of darkness listed in the *Bansenshukai* are actually coded words and jargon in catalog form, to serve as reminders only for qualified members of the ninja family. The words and symbols are intentionally so obscure that only by studying with a legitimate teacher can the student come to know the true meaning of the technique descriptions.

Tenji, the eighth volume, covers the ninja's methods for interpreting and evaluating conditions in the environment. This body of knowledge includes weather forecasting, tide tables, moon phases, and the determination of direction and location by observing the stars. This volume has its basis in generations of experience with systems such as *gogyo setsu* (theory of the five elements), *in-yo do* (taoist principles), and *ekkyo* divination (the *I Ching* Book of Changes), derived from scientific observation and folklore, as well as Indian, Tibetan, and Chinese systems of predicting future trends and happenings.

Ninki, a description of ninja gear, begins in volume nine and continues on into the tenth volume, which is labeled the "tail volume" rather than volume number ten. This is perhaps in keeping with ninjutsu's reliance on the number *9* as a means of inspiration and guidance for enlightenment. The final volume could then be referred to as an additional text, so that the *Bansenshukai* could be said to consist of nine actual volumes.

In the ninth volume, the description of *toki* covers the climbing gear of ninjutsu, and includes a wide variety of equipment that was used to get ninja safely up and down castle walls, trees, cliffs, and ship sides. *Suiki,* based largely on the practical advice from pirates, covers the water gear of ninjutsu. The equipment described provides numerous methods for crossing over or moving under bodies of water. The ninja's *kaiki* is a collection of tools designed for the purpose of breaking into locked or fortified buildings, castles, and storage areas. Pieces of equipment for picking locks, boring through walls, and moving doors are described.

In a manner similar to that used in the description of volume five, six, and seven's combat techniques, the ninja equipment in volume nine is presented with physical dimensions and specifications only. No attempt is made to coach the uninitiated in the proper use of the gear. The *Bansenshukai's* wooden foot gear referred to as *mizugumo* (water spiders) in Andrew Adams' *Ninja, the Invisible Assassins,* for example, are often laughed at for being totally impractical as a means of crossing over the surface of water. What contemporary scoffers do not realize, however, is the fact that the mizugumo were not used to walk across ponds and lakes at all. The foot gear was used to move steadily with a skating action over swampy, marshy areas, flattening out grasses and distributing the ninja's body weight over a broad area of mud, shallow water, and plants, much like snowshoes are used to cross safely over deep drifted snow.

Kaki, referred to as "fire gear," completes the final portion of the *Bansenshukai.* The formulas explained in this tail volume cover the preparation and use of explosives, smoke bombs, medicines, sleeping potions, and poisons. The explicit directions are written in the regional dialect of 17th-century Iga-area Japanese, however, which makes translating a slow and difficult job even for a Japanese person who is schooled in the ancient written forms of the language. For example, local plants are referred to with nicknames of the era and area, so that "bear's paw" indicates an herb and not the foot of the animal. "White horse's breath" would mean a certain blossoming plant, and not the more elusive substance that the name would bring to mind.

The important underlying lessons of history are not to be recognized in the surface manifestations of techniques, strategies, and weapons as described in the *Bansenshukai,* however. The real value and effectiveness of the historical weapons, battle strategies, and communications networks does not lie in the perfection of skills catalogued in a three hundred-year-old reference book series. The lesson is the realization that effective weapons, tools, and means of accomplishment are all around us in everyday articles and situations. If the goal is to be effective in today's surroundings, it will be necessary to leave the antiques in the museum and get involved in what is available today. The historical trappings are fun and remind us of our Japanese ninja heritage, but should not be allowed to become the focus of the training.

Today, authentic Japanese Togakure ryu ninja training is one of the most all-encompassing methods of danger prevention, self-protection, and total living available for study in the world. Historical perspective and creative contemporary applications are blended in the training to provide modern practitioners with a stimulating and inspirational course of self-development that forms the basis for a progressive way of life. Students now train to master the following disciplines:

Junan Taiso	Yoga-like body conditioning exercises
Nin-po taijutsu	Unarmed combat
• *Taihenjutsu*	Body movement, breakfalls, leaping
• *Dakentaijutsu*	Striking and kicking
• *Jutaijutsu*	Grappling and choking
Bojutsu	Staff fighting
Hanbojutsu	Short stick fighting
Ninja ken-po	Fighting with the ninja sword
• *Kenjutsu*	Fencing skills
• *Iaijutsu*	Fast-drawing skills
Tantojutsu	Knife fighting
Shurikenjutsu	Blade throwing
Kusarijutsu	Fighting with short chain weapons
Kyoketsu shoge	Cord and blade weapon
Kusarigama	Chain and sickle weapon
Teppo	Firearms
Ninki	Specialized ninja gear and tools
Fukiya	Blowguns and darts
Heiho	Combat strategy
Gotonpo	Use of natural elements for escape
In-yo do	Taoist principles
Seishin teki kyoyo	Personal clarity
• *Meso*	Meditation
• *Shinpi*	Concepts of mysticism
• *Nin-po mikkyo*	Ninja "secret knowledge" of the universe
Kuji-kiri	Balancing electromagnetic power fields
Kuji-in	Energy channeling

Contemporary practitioners of ninjutsu are by no means limited to the training aspects set forth in the foregoing list, however. Any martial art system, except for a zen-style *do* that is not at all concerned with combat applications, that insists on posting detailed lists of limitations such as *106 weapons* or *42 choking methods* is doing its students a grave disservice by conditioning their minds to think in an orderly structured manner when confronted with danger. With that kind of mechanical training background, the mind will automatically attempt to categorize any new situation by comparing it with previous training examples. Because the mind proudly clings to the 106 weapons notion, it will be natural to overlook the possible combat employment of any object or strategy that did not happen to be included on the list. It should be noted that lists of limitations do, however, make for a neater and more readily packageable martial art system, which provides for more ease in commercializing and marketing the art to buyers.

The authentic ninja art cannot be packaged or systematized easily. The art of ninjutsu exists for the use of the practitioner, and the individual practitioner is not expected to conform to or reduce him or herself to fit the art. For this reason, ninjutsu is not an art that is easily adapted for conventional military training. New recruits have a set period of time in which to learn fundamental skills that they will apply on the job. The open-ended outlook of ninjutsu, along with the art's refusal to set up limiting lists of techniques and the art's emphasis on individual second-to-second analysis of the situation as it unfolds, make it highly unsuitable for troops who will be expected to work as a unit following the commands of a remote leader. The command concept relies on unquestioning obedience; the ninja concept relies on individual intuitive sensitivity and almost unconscious spontaneous decision making.

Ninjutsu has never been a soldier's art. Historically, the ninja usually found themselves opposing soldiers in combat, where they had to use creative imagination and total commitment of intention to overcome the otherwise overwhelming odds. If engaged in any military activity, the ninja's major contribution was as an advisor, a role in which he could apply his unconventional outlooks, his psychic sensitivities, and his physical skills if necessary, in order to balance out the limitations of conventional military thought of the time.

The historical ninja has at best been "misunderstood" by contemporary military and martial arts historians who feel themselves authorities on Japan's feudal era. The samurai are looked up to and praised for their unswerving, undying loyalty to the one lord they served, and their willingness to fling themselves into death unquestioningly for the mere sake of their lord's honor is proudly held up as some sort of example for martial artists even today. Ninja are routinely condemned with accusations of capriciously selling their loyalty to the highest bidder of the moment, and are therefore regarded with disgust as being totally devoid of morality and honor. This type of malicious characterization is usually perpetrated by those writers and historians who wish to glorify the samurai mentality, and does not acknowledge the overexaggerated emphasis placed on group welfare at the expense of the individual in feudal Japanese society.

In truth, the ninja was more loyal to his own family's ideals than to any one human being. The ideal lives on while human beings change with the seasons. What had once been a benevolent and just ruler could become a cruel and greedy tyrant over the years, and the ninja, sensing the ruler's abandonment of the original ideal, would be forced thereby to give his support to other rulers who were more in alignment with the ninja family's philosophy. The samurai on the other hand was taught to avoid questioning the motivations of his superiors and make himself fit for combat only. This code sometimes created the situation in which the samurai knew that his lord or that lord's heir had become a madman, and yet the samurai was still morally obligated by his standards to fight to the death for any whim of the monster that his lord had become.

Certainly, history does have its tales of professional terrorists who would commit any deed for a fee while posing as a ninja. These were, however, desperate wretches who lacked the philosophical foresight and guidance of the major ninja families, and are better described as thugs in black clothing than ninja. Today, contemporary terrorists as well sometimes enjoy claiming kinship to Japan's legendary ninja in an attempt to justify their own irresponsible and brutal behavior. Deluding themselves into believing that they endorse some noble cause, these self-styled night warriors announce to the world that they are championing the fight to stop fascism/communism when in reality they are seeking a rationalization for their own destructive behavior. Neither the self-righteous murderer who blows up hotel lobbies full of tourists in his struggles "for the people," nor the trigger-happy social misfit who hires on to train professional torturers for oppressive dictatorships come anywhere near to carrying on the ways of the ninja. Blurred by heart-twisting hatred or lust for the thrill of violence, the spiritual purity described by Fujibayashi's *Bansenshukai* becomes clouded over with the personal desires that prevent people from acting in accordance with the scheme of totality.

The true ninja is moved to action through love of family and community, and a personal sense of responsibility for the positive channeling of destiny. This motivation cannot be overlooked by anyone researching or studying the art of the ninja. By willfully returning to the unencumbered state of spiritual purity that is possible only through surrendering up those limiting fetters placed on the mind, dedicated practitioners of ninjutsu can come to know the truth that is enlightenment and can then venture between the brightness and darkness unscathed, protected by the universal laws realized through training in the life ways of the ninja. ∎

CHAPTER TWO

There are those misguided persons in the world
*   who would see you harmed.*
They will confront you with fists
*   or await you in the darkness with their blades drawn.*
Do not fear them
*   or become angry with them.*
Allow your heart to hold the emptiness of purity.
Your receptive spirit will hear the sadness and rage
*   of your attackers' intentions*
*   and your body will flow*
*   with the winds of their hatred.*
You will take them to the destruction they seek.

PREPARATION FOR ENCOUNTER
Ninja ways of dealing with danger

T he ninja's combat art is best described as a way of successfully dealing with danger. More than mere self-defense, this ability to live with danger is a total way of life that affects the ninja's outlook on every thing and situation he or she encounters. In most conventional martial systems that stem from samurai origins, practitioners are taught to recognize danger, confront it with training-honed skills, and either triumph over it with humility or be consumed by it with honor. The art of ninjutsu, on the other hand, offers a wider range of possibilities for dealing with potential destruction.

The first and most fundamental approach is to prevent danger from coming into being. Understanding yourself and then extending that understanding to others is the key to making this method work. As a life skill, this involves cultivating the proper attitudes, foresight, and sensitivity that will permit you to consistently be in the right place at the right time. It should be noted that the ninja method of preventing danger is not thought of as a negative or paranoid process in which you always expect the worst and constantly wait or search for it. Quite the contrary, by adopting a positive outlook based on a firm confidence in your abilities to direct your own world, you will find that you can often manipulate elements and events in your environment so far ahead of time that no one but you realizes that anything else could possibly have transpired. Vastly more far reaching in scope than slipping over castle walls in the darkness or out-fighting deadly samurai against normally overwhelming odds, the historical ninja's awesome power to guide the scheme of totality is what originally won Japan's shadow warriors their undisputed respect and fear.

The first lesson: work at setting up your life in such a manner that the enemy never thinks to appear before you. This is realized through developing the spirit.

When the ninja's personal power is not sufficient to prevent the dangerous situation from materializing, the second approach is to successfully endure or outlast the danger. As a life skill, this involves tempering the emotions with the intellect so that threatening situations do not necessarily produce an immediate response, but are evaluated in a detached way so as to determine whether a response is really warranted.

The written Japanese character for *nin* of ninjutsu, nin-po, and ninja (the same character is also pronounced *shinobi* in some usages) has the literal meaning of "endurance, perseverance, or putting-up-with," in both physical and psychological contexts. Whereas the samurai not only had to achieve his aims but also had to accomplish his goals in a more or less accepted and honorable way, the ninja was prevented from having any family house name or honor by the political structure of Japanese society and was thereby free to concentrate his energies on the attainment of his intended goal alone. For this reason the ninja could often allow others to perceive the apparent *appearance* of the ninja's failure or humiliation, when in reality the ninja had attained exactly what he or she had really wanted in the first place. By affecting the perspectives of self and others, the ninja can attain that which is needed without stirring up a desire for retribution, revenge, or defensiveness in others who might provide opposition.

This willfully enduring or appearing to take no action can be more difficult than first imagined. If you are exposed to danger, there is normally a strong feeling of discomfort as long as you are in the presence of the danger. By rising up and overcoming the danger, you eliminate the threat and thereby return to a relaxed or relieved state. Conquering the danger, whatever it may have been, might not have been the most appropriate action to have taken, however, if it exposes your position and opens you up to increased danger. It is far more difficult to endure the danger without tension, to dwell impassively in the very shadow of death, taking no action that will give away your intentions, and allowing the danger to go its own way leaving you unharmed and untouched.

The second lesson: work at transcending your emotions so that you do not always automatically respond with a defense even when a defense is not needed. This is realized through developing the mind.

When the ninja has not been able to guide the happenings of fate in order to prevent danger, and has not been able to allow the danger to pass by without effect, actual defensive tactics will then be necessary. Physical combat methods usually come to mind first, rather than third, for many people when they think of ninjutsu as a martial art. In actuality, however, physically coming to grips with danger is the least preferable method of returning life to harmony and naturalness, in that it involves the greatest potential risk of something going wrong.

Nonetheless, contemporary ninja training usually begins with physical lessons, because a solid grounding in physical reality is a prerequisite for any valid intellectual or spiritual growth. The techniques of hand-to-hand or weapon combat can then serve as models for understanding the effects of the mind, emotions, and spirit on the outcome of a conflict or confrontation.

The third lesson: work at perfecting the skills for successfully handling physical violence directed against you. This is realized through developing the body.

The physical self-defense elements of ninjutsu blend a wide range of natural body weapons and combat tools into a single comprehensive total fighting art. Whether *dakentaijutsu* striking techniques, *bojutsu* stick fighting techniques, or *shurikenjutsu* throwing-blade techniques are being employed, the body moves with identical footwork, dynamics, and energy direction. Merely replacing a fist with a short club does not alter the ninja's way of moving in the fight. Substituting a sword blade for a sweeping kick does not at all change the feeling of the ninja's technique as it unfolds.

In essence, the ninja combat method is more accurately described as a series of feelings rather than a collection of technqiues. Because all bodies and personalities are unique, no attempt is made to coerce the practitioners of ninjutsu into imitating or taking on one rigid standard set of movements. Instead, guidelines are provided to encourage the most effective use and application of all the natural emotional and physical reactions that occur during a conflict or confrontation.

Having its foundations in the tantric lore of northern India and Tibet, the doctrine of nin-po *mikkyo* (secret knowledge) teaches that all physical aspects of existence originate from a common source and can be classified in one of the *godai* five elemental manifestations of physical matter. *Chi*, or the earth, symbolizes solid matter. *Sui*, the water, symbolizes liquids. *Ka*, the fire, is the symbol of combustion, or the elements in an energy-releasing state. *Fu*, the wind, symbolizes gases. *Ku*, the void, is representative of the formless subatomic energy that is the basis for the structure of all things. This godai symbolism is also used to describe the emotional nature of human beings, and to provide a symbolic structure for the teaching of effective physical combat principles in ninjutsu.

The godai five elements provide a series of symbolic codes that can be used to describe the varying ways in which we all respond to direct confrontation. The chi earth influence is seen in the stability or stubbornness of the personality, and is also acted out by the fighter who firmly holds his ground and overcomes attackers through unvacillating presence and strength. The sui water influence is seen in the flexibility or emotionalism of the personality, and is also demonstrated by the fighter who uses defensive angling and footwork to overextend his attacker to the point where his power is sufficient for an effective counterattack. The ka fire influence is seen in the natural aggressiveness and fear of the personality, and is displayed by the fighter who uses direct energetic attacks as defenses in a combat clash. Fu, the wind influence, shows up as the wisdom and love in the personality, and is reflected in evasive, elusive fighting methods that redirect the attacker's movements away from their targets. Ku, the fifth element, is the creative, communicative aspects of the personality, and absolute spontaneity and inventiveness when applied in a fight.

The following examples help to characterize the physical, emotional, perceptual, mechanical, and intellectual relationships of the five elemental manifestation code labels.

Emotional responses

Earth	You are the junior high school principal confronted by a thirteen-year-old troublemaker who did not expect you to come upon him. Your natural feeling is one of total power that can handle all and that needs to fear nothing.

Water	You are alone on a deserted night subway, when a huge, rough looking thug enters your car and heads right for you with a surly leer on his face. Your natural feeling is one of total defensiveness.
Fire	You are confronted by the teenager who gave your young daughter such a savage beating that she was hospitalized in a coma. Your natural feeling is one of pure aggressive rage that causes you to forget any concern for yourself.
Wind	A beloved relative has had too much to drink and violently confronts you over a misunderstanding. Your natural feeling is one of compassion that provides a sufficient defense without a retaliation or counterattack.

Physical center of tension and movement

Earth	Thighs and seat
Water	Lower abdomen, navel
Fire	Solar plexus
Wind	Center of chest, heart

Source of body dynamics

Earth	Strength
Water	Power
Fire	Energy
Wind	Resiliency

Adversary's perception of your fighting actions

Earth	Nothing affects you or hurts you. You are immoveable.

Water	You seem unreachable, and yet when reached you are always ready with a counterattack.
Fire	You cannot be stopped. There is no chance to get anything in on you.
Wind	You are slippery, always disappearing and causing the original attack to backfire against its application.

Characteristic body vibrations

Earth	Up and down
Water	Side to side
Fire	Forward and backward
Wind	Rotating on spinal axis

Characteristic footwork

Earth	Feet firmly in place; immoveable
Water	Backpedaling zig-zag angling away from attack
Fire	Forward moving shuffle or run; applying pressure
Wind	Circular, sidestepping, and slipping evasions

Each of the elemental manifestation codes can be seen reflected in the body postures employed in the ninja's fighting method. The postures, or *kamae,* are assumed naturally as the body goes through the realization that combative action is necessary. Each fighting posture, whether employed for unarmed defense, sword or blade fighting, stick techniques, or methods employing the chain and cord weapons, is a physical manifestation of the emotions, attitude, and mental set.

For a fuller understanding of the application philosophy of ninjutsu's fighting postures, which are actually temporary bases from which to launch techniques, it is crucial to remember that the postures are never used as static poses or stances. Using the printed format of a book, it is impossible to effectively depict the vibrancy, energy, and dynamism that are the very life of the ninjutsu kamae in combat. A photograph on a page gives the inaccurate impression that the posture is to be held continuously as the ninja moves about in combat. Quite the contrary, in real combat, the postures are assumed for mere seconds as they become necessary and then are just as quickly dropped when their effectiveness has passed. As a parallel, a photograph of a ninja in one of the fighting postures could be compared to a photograph of a basketball player suspended in midair as he completes a dunk shot. We would no more expect the basketball player to continuously hold his midair pose than we would expect the ninja to freeze into one of his combat poses. The feet continuously work to alter the ninja's distancing, angling, and positioning.

Earth Element

Unarmed Natural Posture
(taijutsu shizen no kamae)

Unarmed "Immoveable" Seat
(taijutsu fudo za)

Sword Kneeling Seat
(kenjutsu seiza)

Short Chain Looped Through
Belt Ready for Drawing
(kusarifundo shizen no kamae)

Short Stick Natural Posture
(hanbojutsu shizen no kamae)

Water Element

Unarmed Defensive Posture
(taijutsu ichimonji no kamae)

Unarmed "Tiger" Defensive Posture
(taijutsu doko no kamae)

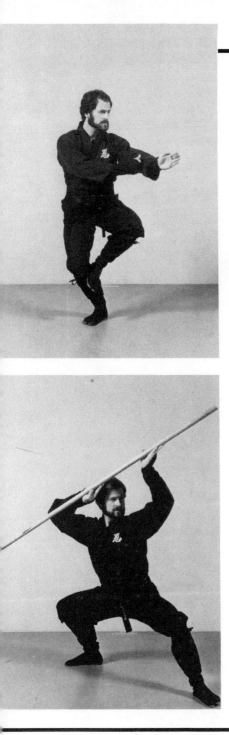

Unarmed "Crane" Defensive Posture
(taijutsu hicho no kamae)

Sword Level Defensive Posture
(kenjutsu ichi no kamae)

Staff High Blocking Posture
(bojutsu jodan uke no kamae)

Fire Element

Unarmed Offense Posture
(taijutsu jumonji no kamae)

Unarmed Attacking Posture
(taijutsu kosei no kamae)

Sword High Striking Posture
(kenjutsu jodan no kamae)

Staff Middle Striking Posture
(bojutsu chudan no kamae)

Short Chain Striking Posture
(kusarifundo ichi no kamae)

Wind Element

Unarmed Receiving Posture
(taijutsu hira no kamae)

Unarmed "Bear" Open Posture
(taijutsu hoko no kamae)

Staff "Heaven and Earth" Posture
(bojutsu techi no kamae)

Sword "Water Willow" Posture
(kenjutsu ryusui no kamae)

Short Chain Receiving Posture
(kusarifundo hira no kamae)

CHAPTER THREE

Just as the tangled grasses
take over the mountainside
and the roots of the pines
split clusters of boulders,
the ninja's inventiveness and creative outlook
easily defeat the immobilized enemy
trapped in his own morass
of ponderous narrow vision.

TAIHENJUTSU
Ninja methods of rebounding from the ground

The unarmed combat techniques of ninjutsu are referred to as *tai-jutsu* (skill with the body). As subclassifications within the broad category of fighting without artificial weapons, there are three major groupings of techniques. *Dakentaijutsu* striking methods employ *koppojutsu* bone smashes with the fist and bottom of the foot, and *koshijut-su* organ and muscle stabs with the fingers and toes. *Jutaijutsu* grappling methods employ *nage* throws, *shime* chokes, and *torite* close-in reversals

and locks. *Taihenjutsu,* the body movement skills that make up the third major subclass, include *ukemi* methods of breaking falls, *tobi* leaps, *taisabaki* body angling, and *shinobi iri* silent movement.

Though rarely taught in the vast majority of martial arts schools in the western world, the skills of hitting the ground safely and rebounding ready to continue the fight or escape swiftly are crucial for the mastery of a truly combat-oriented fighting art. Real world self-protection goes far beyond the rules and limitations enjoyed by participants engaged in contemporary recreational martial arts programs. To be truly combat ready, today's martial artist must be prepared and trained not only to fight the conventional standing fist fight, but also to be able to fight from a station wagon front seat, the floor of a broom closet, in the middle of a chair-packed diner, and on the way down a flight of fire-escape stairs. Total self-protection capabilities would also have to include successfully tumbling from a moving truck, going over a high wall to avoid an attack dog, and flattening out on a floor surface to avoid being hit by gunfire.

The ninja taihenjutsu techniques are first taught as slow-motion fundamentals from a low crouched position on a protective mat. Principles of lowering the center of gravity, exhaling with movement, and relaxing the body are emphasized. Once the feel of the techniques is acquired, practice is moved to grassy outdoor stretches for increased realism. As the practitioner's skills mature, training then moves to asphalt road surfaces, staircases, and other actual locations where the skills will be required in real life defensive combat.

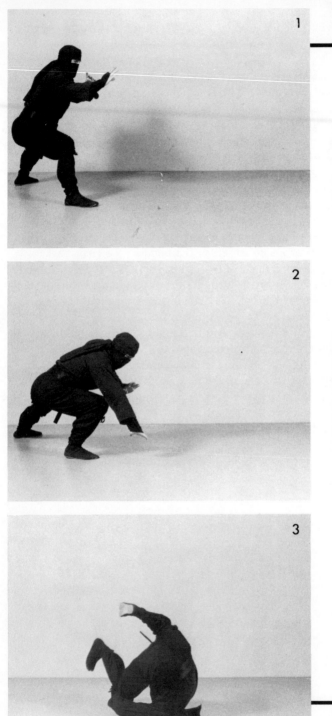

THE FORWARD ROLL

The forward roll is used to accommodate offensive techniques that throw or pull the defender forward onto the ground. The natural movement and energy of

Forward Roll

From an unarmed defensive posture (1) allow your body frame (2) to form an arch that begins with the extended leading arm and shoulder. Tuck your head down and rock forward briskly (3) allowing your

the attacker's technique is enhanced and carried through by curling the body, so that the defender ends up on his feet again instead of on his face and chest.

body weight to roll onto your arm, across your shoulder and (4) over your hips. Keep your feet tucked in and (5) continue the rolling motion to (6) come back up onto your feet.

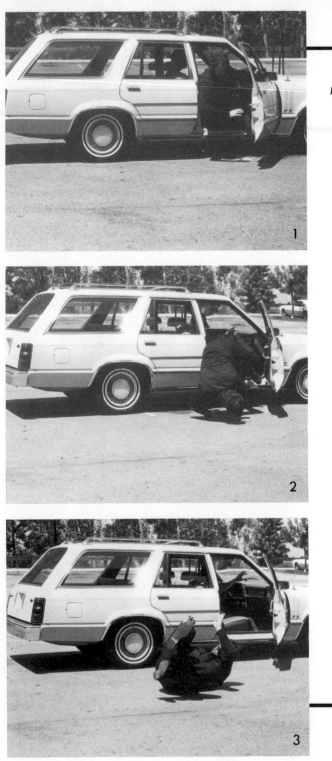

1

2

3

4

5

6

THE BACKWARD ROLL

The backward roll is used to accommodate techniques in which the attacker throws or pulls the defender backwards on to the ground. The natural movement and energy of the attacker's

Backward Roll

From an unarmed defensive posture (1) step back and (2) drop to the ground in as direct a manner as possible. Arch your back and bring your head down

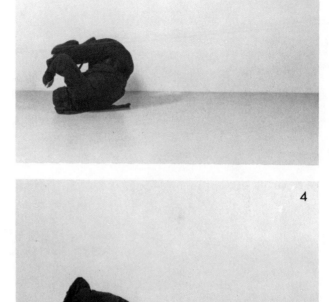

technique is enhanced and carried through by dropping the seat and tucking the legs, so that the defender ends up on his feet again instead of his back.

to your upper chest while (3) allowing your rolling momentum to continue. Keep your feet tucked in and (4&5) roll right up onto your feet.

THE FORWARD HANDSPRING

The forward handspring is one method of accommodating offensive techniques that knock or send the defender forward. The weight is flipped on to the outstretch-

Forward Handspring

From a (1) standing position, dive out (2) so that your body weight sinks down onto your bending arms. Your elbows and shoulders (3) should flex to accommodate your moving weight. Immediately (4) push back against your

ed arms, and the body flexes to send the feet forward over the head. The defender then bounces up from the ground to regain his footing.

lowering weight while kicking forward (the direction of travel) with both upraised feet. Flex your back in an arch (5) to snap your hips after your feet. Finally (6) follow the lead of your feet and straighten out into a standing position.

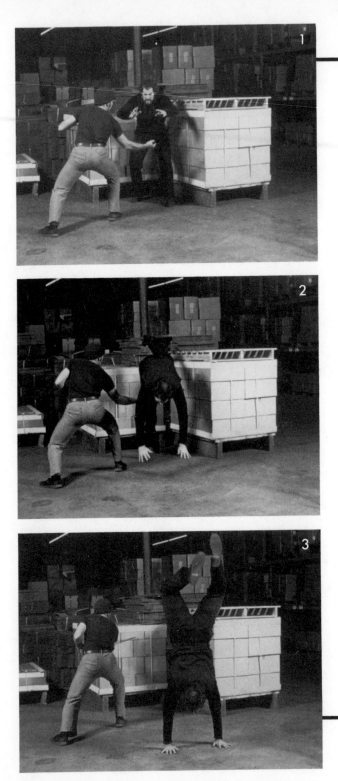

THE SIDEWAYS HANDSPRING

The sideways handspring accommodates an attacker's technique that knocks or sends the defender sideways. The weight is leaned side-

Sideways Handspring

From an unarmed defensive posture (1) leap out to the side (2) while lowering your leading shoulder. As your extended hand hits the ground (3) kick off with your feet to propel your hips up and over your

ways, and the body flips to send the feet to the side over the head. The defender then cartwheels up from the ground to regain his footing.

shoulders. Extend your limbs widely so that the rolling action will cover as wide an area as possible. The sideways momentum (4&5) should pull your body back up onto your feet again.

Sideways Leap

From an unarmed receiving posture (1) slam your hips in the direction of travel (2) pushing off with your trailing leg and clearing your leading leg by picking it up. Keep the leap as level as possible (3) moving directly sideways without bounding up and down with the move. The

action should center in the legs and hips and take the upper body along. Do not throw your shoulders to get your body in motion. Then (4) as you land on your leading leg, plant both feet on the ground and (5) assume the unarmed receiving posture once again.

Lateral Body Drop

From an unarmed receiving posture (1) center your body weight on one foot (2) and swing your free leg across in front of your ground leg. Then (3) lower your seat directly to the ground. Lift your extended leg up which will flip your

body (4) over onto your back. Continue to "reach" with your extended leg (5) until both feet are again (6) in touch with the ground. Allow your rolling motion to move you into a standing position again.

CHAPTER FOUR

The steel from the earth
  and the wood from the forest
  are tempered by the fire
  and washed in the stream for purity
  to become the servants
  of the winds of your intention.
Use your weapons with prudence,
  employing them only when
  the scheme of totality demands it.

TRAINING FOR COMBAT REALITY
Ninjutsu methods for overcoming attackers

T he constantly evolving combat method of togakure ryu ninjutsu allows for changes and developments in the ways that people are likely to attack. Based on a timeless understanding of human attitudes and physiology that far transcends the rigid limits of temporally inspired techniques, all of the ninja fighting methods serve as practical, reliable routes of self-protection that utilize the natural physical and emotional response tendencies of the human being. This practicality must be present as the core philosophy of any combat effective fighting system.

It should be remembered that the art of ninjutsu was not developed or practiced for the sake of the art itself, nor were there any symbolic goals such as belt rankings or sports titles involved. Ninjutsu developed as a utilitarian and dependable method for accomplishing personal intentions with the least possible amount of personal danger.

The emphasis in ninja training is not on the techniques themselves, but rather on the feelings that come up during application of the techniques. Practice sessions, whether inside the dojo or outside in natural surroundings, freely blend the methods of unarmed combat, stick fighting, blade work, and short cord techniques to produce the feeling of a total system, rather than independent blocks of knowledge for each specialty. This teaching method admittedly requires more time for mastery, because the personality is internalizing concepts by stripping away false or unnecessary intellectualizations, rather than the intellect memorizing set numbers of compartmentalized techniques.

There are two sides to the learning process involved in developing skill in self-protection fighting: the mind and the body. The first aspect of the training is to develop an unconscious, spontaneous mind and body response to an attack. This by no means suggests rigid programmed reactions of a "strike and then think" nature, but rather a natural and relaxed response that is developed through repetitive practice that removes the need for conscious logical steps. This unconscious action can be seen as you head a sports car up an incline, discover that it is becoming increasingly steep, work the clutch and accelerator with your feet, and downshift to ease the strain on the engine, all without deliberate conscious involvement. The second aspect of training is the exposure to the experience of effective and appropriate defensive techniques. The physical techniques themselves are important, of course, as they are the entire method of practice during the training session and they will condition you for later response during self-protection. However, the mental and spiritual conditioning is the highest goal of the training, as without the proper mental set, even the most devastating of techniques will not be recalled when they are needed.

As a guide for effective ninjutsu training, it is crucial to understand the significance of the following considerations.

1. *Be there 100 percent. Allow your consciousness to hold on to each moment as though it were all that existed. Concentrate totally on your purpose and actions.*
   Do not let your mind wander from the training activities at hand.

2. *Keep your center of gravity as low as possible while still permitting easy movement.*
   Do not concentrate your strength in your shoulders or upper body.

3. *Keep your movements relaxed and fluid, delivering the impact at the last second.*

Do not tense up by trying to maintain power through the entire technique.

4. *Use the entire weight of the body to create power and knock your attacker back or down.*
Do not try to out-muscle the attacker with the movements of your limbs alone.

5. *Keep your footwork fast, responsive, and appropriate.*
Do not settle into and maintain a fixed stance for the fight.

6. *Use proper rhythmic breathing to generate and restore energy. Breathe out with application movements and in with retreating or preparation movements.*
Do not hold your breath when releasing energy through technique application or interception.

7. *Control the direction of your eyes, keeping your attacker in sight.*
Do not concentrate so much on your technique that you do not notice a possible change in the attacker's action or position.

8. *Bear in mind the purpose of the technique.*
Do not attempt to carry through a technique that is no longer needed. (If the attacker lets go before you can complete the wrist lock, that's fine. Your purpose was to get him off of you, not execute a textbook technique.)

9. *Use every moment to increase your personal knowledge and powers.*
Do not merely go through the motions for the sake of exercise or forced discipline.

The following examples are provided as illustrations of ninja combat method training. The techniques are not necessarily to be memorized, but rather serve as guidelines for understanding the principles. The ultimate goal is not to memorize dozens of robot-like series movements, but to strip away the attachments of the intellectual mind. If your fighting ability is based on memorized techniques, then time and human forgetfulness will decrease your fighting ability if you even temporarily discontinue active training. If on the other hand, your fighting ability is the product of stripping away and letting go of all the mechanical thought processes that limit the mind, you will have nothing to lose through forgetfulness. You will have transcended the need for constant uninterrupted training, and you will have realized the essence of "being" rather than "becoming."

Single-Hand Choke Escape I

From a ready position (1) the attacker (2) has grabbed the defender by the throat. The defender (3) responds by going with the attacking pressure. (*Note:* (A) shows the correct hand position for dislodging the attacker's hand.) She steps back into a stable defensive posture while (4) dislodging the attacker's

hand. Continuing back with her footwork, (5) the defender twists out against the attacker's wrist to (6) throw him to the ground. (*Note:* (B) shows the correct hand position at this point.) The defender uses her body weight in motion, and not her arms alone, to down the attacker.

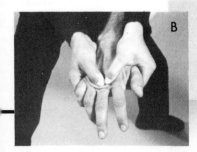

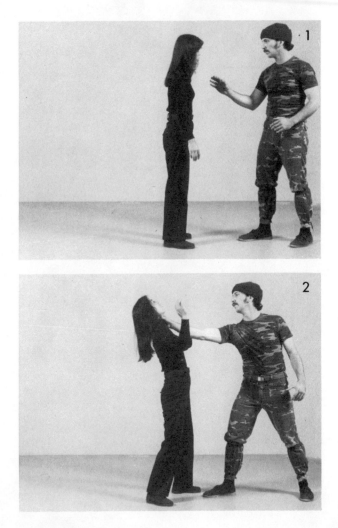

Single-Hand Choke Escape II

From a ready position (1) the attacker has grabbed the defender by the throat. The defender (2&3) by go-

ing with the attacker's pressure steps back into a defensive posture (4) while freeing the attacker's

Continued on next page

6

7

hand. Continuing back with her footwork (5&6) the defender pulls the attacker's wrist inward with a twist to (7-9) throw him to the ground.

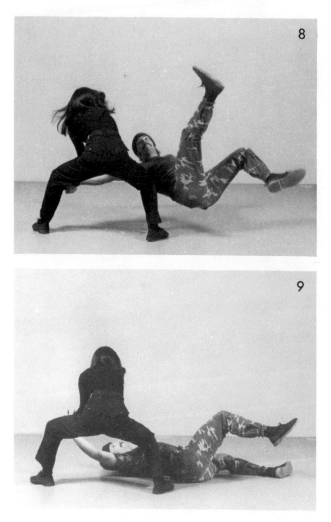

Defense Against a Redirected Attack

From a defensive posture (1) the defender observes as the attacker (2) moves forward with a front hand punch to the face. In response (3) the defender throws his leading foot to the outside rear position and (4) counterpunches in-

to the attacker's extended punching arm. The attacker recoils his arm with the power of the defender's strike, and allows the momentum of his body to turn him (5&6) into a spinning back kick to the defender's

Continued on next page

midsection. As the kick rises toward him (7) the defender counters by kicking into the back of the attacking leg. As the attacker's leg is pushed to the ground again (8) he goes with the spin to (9) ex-

ecute a rear hammer-fist strike to the defender's head. The defender drops to avoid the strike and then (10&11) steps in with a throat-crushing grip that (12) slams the attacker back and up.

Defense Against Punching Attack

From a defensive posture (1) the defender observes as the attacker (2) executes a hooking knockout punch to the head. Once the punch is committed to its path (3) the defender drops straight down to avoid being hit. The move is a body drop, not a boxer's duck. From

the grounded position (4) the defender springs back up toward the attacker, using her legs to generate power. As she rises (5) the defender shifts her rear leg into forward position, increasing the power of her punch (6) to the attacker's lower ribs. The completed

Continued on next page

punch uses the defender's body weight in motion to deliver power, rather than the simple extension of her arm. The defender then shuffles forward (7-9) with a rising shin kick to the groin and (10&11) a heel stamp to the knee. Since the defender's arm mus-

cles are not as strong as the attacker's, she must overcome his strength by avoiding his strikes and using her whole body for the counterstrike. Finally (12) the defender completes the maneuver with a heel stamp to the back of the attacker's leg.

Knife Defense Against Knife Attack I

From a receiving posture (1) the defender observes as the attacker (2) closes in with horizontal slashing cuts to her hands and mid-section. As the attacker slashes inward with a pulling cut, the defender allows her body to fall back momentarily and then (3) rocks forward with an outward hacking cut to the outside edge of the attacker's weapon arm. As the

blade wedges into its target (4) the defender moves forward to use her body weight and position to prevent the attacker from slashing back at her. Continuing her momentum, (5) the defender moves directly behind the attacker, leveling out her knife so that her body weight in motion, not the muscles in her arm alone, (6) drives the knife into its target.

Knife Defense Against Knife Attack II

From a receiving posture (1) the defender observes as the attacker closes in with horizontal slashing cuts to her hands and mid-section (2). As the attacker slashes outward with a pushing cut, the defender allows her body to fall back momentarily and then without hesitation (3) rocks forward while simultaneously grabbing the attacker's weapon arm and executing a downward slicing cut to the inside of the

attacker's upper arm. The defender then (4) continues the momentum of her blade as it passes underneath the attacker's arm, and then (5) swings her blade up into position to control the attacker by holding him in a defenseless position. If necessary to save her own life (6) the defender could then cut downward along the attacker's neck from behind his shoulder.

Defense Against a Double Punch Attack

From a defensive posture (1) the defender observes as the attacker begins a double face punch combination. The defender (2) shifts back and to the inside of the first punch with an injurious counterstrike to the attacking arm. As the attacker recoils (3) and then dives in with his second punch (4) the defender shifts her body weight forward into an offensive pos-

ture and causes the attacker to slam his chest into the point of her elbow. The attacker's second punch misses its target, due to the defender's sudden and unexpected change in movement. The defender (5) then executes a clawing hand strike to the face, followed by an outside arm lock (6) which forces the attacker to the ground.

Defense Against a Combination Attack

From a defensive posture (1) the defender observes as the attacker (2&3) executes a leg-sweeping kick. As the attacker's leg shoots out, the defender (4)

lifts his foot to avoid the strike. The attacker immediately (5) flies forward with a leading-hand punch to the defender's ribs. As a

Continued on next page

counter (6) the defender smashes down with his leading fist and (7&8) uses his coiled leg to kick forward into the attacker's midsection. The defender

(9) then moves into an offensive posture as he (10& 11) knocks the attacker back with a palm-edge strike to the side of the neck.

Defense Against Wall Pin

The attacker (1-3) slams the defender up against a wall. As the attacker shoves, the defender arches his back and lowers his head forward to cushion the impact. The defender then (4) allows his body to fall forward as the attacker (5) initiates a face punch. By lowering his center of gravity and moving forward, the defender jams up the attack. The defender (6&7) next extends his arm over the grabbing arm of the attacker, allows his arm to swing down and around, and drops his body weight to trap the attacker's arm from above. By turning his body into the attack and continuing the swing of his arm, the defender exerts straining pressure on the outside of the attacker's elbow and shoulder, (8) which

2

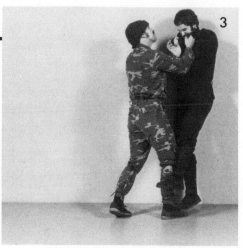

3

5

6

8

Continued on next page

Continued from previous page

turns the attacker's body to prevent his punch from connecting. The defender then simultaneously lifts up on the elbow, drops his seat and (9) leans back, which slams the attacker backwards into the wall. The defender next (10) regrips the attacker's body, lowers his seat once again and (11&12) slings the attacker forward into the wall. Knee slam follow-up strikes (13&14) disable the attacker's legs and bring the fight (15&16) to a close.

10

11

13

14

16

Defense to Offense Transition

From an offensive posture (1) the defender is preparing to go from defense into offense against the attacker. As the defender begins his move, the attacker (2)

3

4

flies forward with a punch to the face. The defender (3&4) drops to the inside of the attacker's punch and directs his fist into the underside of the attacker's

5

Continued on next page

6

7

extended arm. Then (5&6) quickly trapping the attacker's foot with his own foot, the defender (7) rams forward with a thumb-drive strike to the attacker's up-

8

9

per ribs, stunning him and knocking him back. Finally (8-10) two-handed pressure on the attacker's knees forces him to the ground or breaks his ankle.

10

Defense Against Redirected Attack

From a defensive posture (1) the defender observes as the attacker (2) initiates a front hand jab. The defender (3) shifts to the rear and side to avoid the jab and counters with a speed

punch to the attacker's leading wrist. The counter is actually an attack from the defensive posture, and not a block. As the attacker continues (4&5) with a lunging punch to the ribs,

Continued on next page

the defender (6) rocks forward and to the outside of the punch and uses her leading hand to redirect the punch. The defender (7-9) then rams her knee in-

to the bone structure of the attacker's leg and follows up (10) with an extended knuckle punch into the bones of the attacker's ribs or neck.

Metsubushi *Defense Against Sword*

From a receiving posture, (1) the defender observes as the attacker (2) prepares to execute a slashing cut with his sword. The defender retreats into a de-

fensive posture as the attacker raises his sword. From a concealed pocket inside her jacket (3) the defender produces a packet

Continued on next page

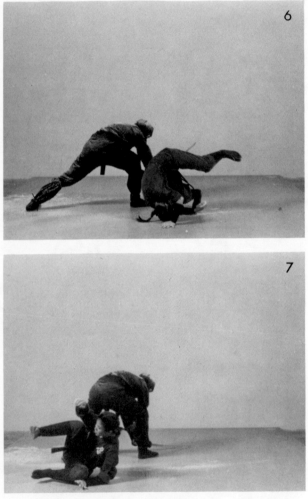

of *metsubushi* (blinding powder) which (4) she throws into the eyes of the attacker. As the attacker

attempts to complete his blind cut (5-9) the defender escapes by rolling past the attacker unseen.

Sword Versus Sword I

From a natural posture (1) the defender observes as the attacker approaches. As soon as the attacker reaches for his sword (2) the defender draws his sword while moving forward into an offensive posture. The thumb of the left hand presses the guard to free the blade from its scabbard. The defender (3&4) turns his drawing action into his

first cut against the attacker's arm. Properly executed, this move is totally an attack. There is no hesitation or defensiveness about it. After the first cut (5&6) the defender continues forward with a downward slashing cut to finish off the attacker. The body weight in motion carries the blade into its target. The cut is not propelled by arms alone.

Sword Versus Sword II

From a seated position (1) the defender observes as the attacker moves into position before him with sword upraised. Staring into the attacker's eyes, the defender uses his left hand to subtly reverse the position of his sword to edge-

down in his sash. Then (2-4) staying low, the defender bursts forward with a fast-draw upward, ripping cut as the attacker moves in with his downward cut. The defender's move is totally an attack with no defensive hesitation about it at

Continued on next page

all. The defender then continues forward (5-9) slamming his body weight into a horizontal cut across the

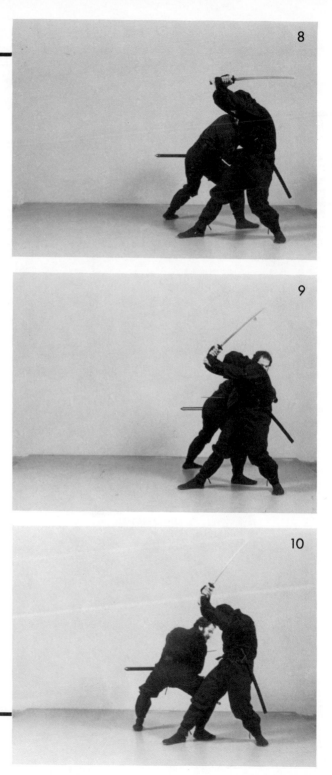

attacker's midsection (10) while moving to the side to avoid the attacker's falling sword.

Unarmed Defense
Against a Knife I

From a receiving posture (1) the defender observes as the attacker moves in with a vertically plunging knife stab along the neck and behind the collarbone. Instead of recoiling back

predictably, the defender (2-4) moves forward along the outside of the attacker's descending knife arm, (5) guiding it away with his own leading hand. Captur-

Continued on next page

Continued from previous page

ing the attacker's momentum, the defender then extends the attacker's knife arm and subdues him with

knee smashes to (6&7) the back of the elbow and (8&9) a heel stamp to the side of the knee.

Unarmed Defense Against a Knife II

From a receiving posture (1) the unarmed defender observes as the attacker uses a knife to hold him at bay with short slashes and lunges. The attacker (2) charges forward with an upward stab to the lower tip of the defender's breastbone. The defender (3&4) adapts by flowing for-

ward and outside of the attacker's knife arm, using his leading hand to stabilize the attacking arm. Immediately (5-7) the defender grips the attacker's knife wrist and steps forward with an extended knuckle attack to the bones in the back of the attacker's knife hand. The

Continued on next page

6

7

defender's body weight in motion provides the power to stun the attacker's hand, and the blade will usually fly free. The defender (8&9) then turns against the attacker's wrist, using his body

8

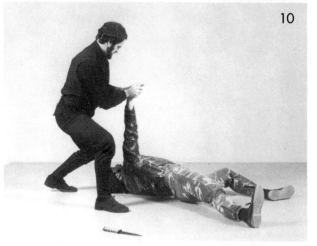

weight to snap the wrist and throw the attacker to the ground on his back. The final maneuver (10&11) is to twist the attacker's wrist to the right to keep him under control.

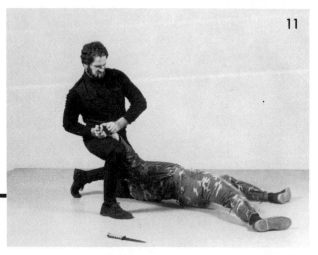

Sword Versus Sword III

From a defensive posture (1) the defender observes as the attacker (2) lunges forward with a downward diagonal cut. The defender then (3&4) throws his sword forward to meet the blade of the attacker with-

out attempting to stop his motion. As the attacker's sword continues forward (5&6) the defender allows his own sword to fall away with it, firmly guiding (not blocking) the attacking

Continued on next page

Continued from previous page

blade from its target. After the attacker's power is no longer a threat (7&8) the defender releases his sword with his leading hand and grabs the attacker's jacket sleeve to

keep him from turning with another cut. The defender then (9) lowers his own sword point into a position where he can control the attacker's movement.

Shuriken Defense Against Sword

From a defensive posture (1) the defender observes as the attacker (2) moves forward with a slashing attack. The defender (3&4) throws his leading foot back with a leap to avoid

the cut. As he backpedals away from the attacker (5) the defender reaches into his jacket and produces a stack of nine *shuriken* throwing stars. As the at-

Continued on next page

tacker bears down on him (6-10) the defender fires off several of the blades to drive the attacker back. (*Note:* (A), (B), (C) and (D) show the correct technique for throwing the shuriken

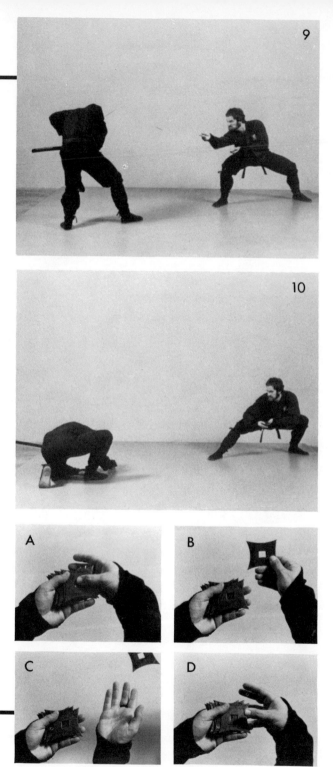

in rapid-fire succession. The throwing stars are fanned off the top of the stack one at a time very quickly, the hand snapping back for the next blade as soon as the first one is thrown.)

Short Chain
Against Club

From a defensive posture (1) the defender observes as the attacker approaches with an iron club. As the club moves into position for a downward smashing strike to the head or shoulder (2) the defender moves forward into an offensive posture and meets the descending club hand

with the taut chain. Holding the clubbing hand in place temporarily with the chain (3-5) the defender moves to the attacker's side (away from the attacker's free hand) from which position the defender can tie the attacker's clubbing hand against his own neck.

Continued on next page

The chain then (6-8) wraps around the attacker's neck and the defender's right thumb applies the choking pressure to the attacker's windpipe. Finally (9) the defender pulls the attacker to the ground.

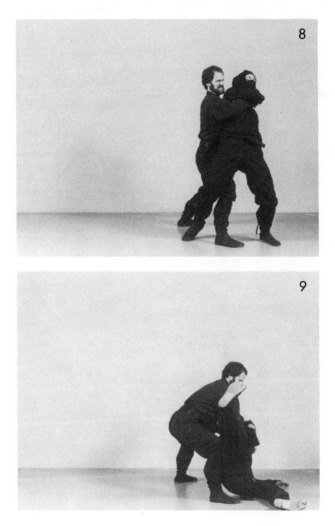

Knife Versus Stick

From a defensive posture (1) the defender observes as the attacker (2) approaches with short, slashing knife work. The defend-

er (3&4) rocks forward into an offensive posture and sends the tip of his cane into the knife hand of the attacker. The defender con-

Continued on next page

6

7

tinues his forward motion (5-7) using his body weight and natural speed to generate power as he releases

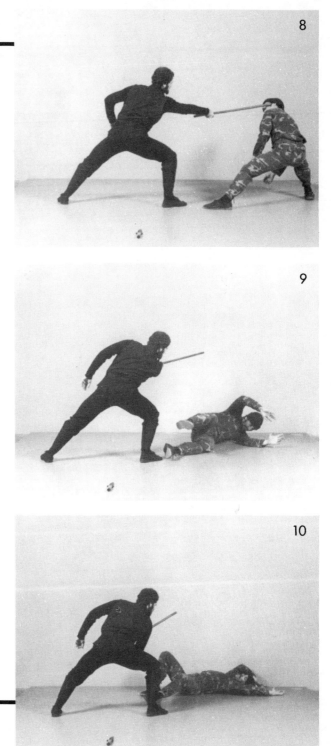

his rear gripping hand (8-10) to send the cane forward into the attacker's face.

Stick Defense Against Staff Attack

From a defensive posture (1) the defender observes as the attacker (2) flies forward with a diagonal staff strike to the head or neck. In response (3) the defender moves in to stop the attacking motion, and then (4) uses his leading arm to

control the attacker's staff. Lowering his body weight for power (5) the defender cracks the tip of the short stick into the attacker's temple (6) knocking him unconscious as he tumbles to the ground.

NORTH

WEST

The Taizokai Mandala

CHAPTER FIVE

The fingers interwoven
  to channel the determination,
  a tensing of the bones and muscles,
  passage of the breath
  and setting of the resolve
  propel the ninja
  to seize and ride the winds of fate.

ATTUNING WITH THE UNIVERSE
Thought, word, and deed as a single tool of accomplishment for the ninja: *Kuji-in*

n his volume entitled *Nin-po: Sono Hiden to Jitsurei* (Secrets and Examples of the Ninja Ways), now no longer in print, Iga ryu ninjutsu historian Heishichiro Okuse observes that Japan's historical ninja are characterized by their thorough and scientific approach to analyzing and solving problems, and yet they are at the same time closely associated with highly occult and spiritual practices. From Okuse's viewpoint, this is really no contradiction at all. Ninja combat training tends to stress the pragmatic physical aspects in precise and rational ways with little or no attention paid to artistic or aesthetic considerations, but the ninja of old also realized that a lot of their successes came through influences other than scientific predetailing of operations to be undertaken. Some persons would call these subtle influences luck, coincidence, or accident, but the ninja learned that a rational and logical approach had to rationally and logically include all factors that could possibly influence an outcome.

Ninjutsu's reliance on the practice of *mikkyo* stressed the truth of the concepts that there is no such thing as coincidence, there are no accidents, and luck is just unguided or unchanneled power playing itself out in our daily affairs. This conviction that spirituality is a legitimate and working part of reality comes from a heightened sensitivity resulting from continuously dwelling on the border edge between life and death. To a veteran ninja who has lived through countless skirmishes against overwhelming odds and has seen too many unexplainable happenings and miraculous twists of fate, there is nothing more rational than taking all possibilities into account.

From the mystic teachings of mikkyo came the ninja's insight into the workings of the universe, and from the application of this understanding came the ninja's personal power. The compendium of wisdom teachings known as mikkyo had its foundations in the esoteric tantric lore of India, Tibet, and China. In the early part of the ninth century, Japan was introduced to these concepts through the research of traveling monks such as Saicho and Kukai, who traveled to China as young men in order to study with learned sages there. Mikkyo teachings of power and magic also came to Japan through the work of wandering monks, shamans, and hermit priests who fled their native China after the fall of the T'ang Dynasty.

In later centuries, the same teachings underwent a stylization and elaboration in their native India and Tibet, and were transformed into a religion of worship and adoration of a spectrum of gods that represented the varying levels of consciousness in the universe. In feudal Japan, however, the teachings were transmitted as a body of knowledge that stressed the power inherent in every individual person. Not merely a religion, but a working set of principles or universal laws, the teachings of mikkyo were taken to heart and practiced rigorously by *yamabushi, sennin,* and *gyoja* mountain warrior ascetics, the segment of Japanese society that would later become the forerunners of the ninja. In a series of brutal religious and territorial wars, these people were hunted down for holding views contrary to the state religion at the time. The need for defense of their mountain wilderness homes, families, and beliefs soon developed, and thus was born the incredible shadow warrior of Japan, known as the ninja.

NINJA

In modern Japan, the mikkyo teachings are now an elaborate religion, considered to be the tantric or esoteric side of Buddhism. The methods of Saicho became known as the *Tendai* sect over the centuries, while the teachings of Kukai (later known by the posthumous name of Kobo Daishi, or "great teacher of the universal laws"), which were perhaps closer to the original *shugenja* beliefs of the ninja, became formalized as *Shingon* Buddhism. These forms of mikkyo, with their ornate trappings and complex rituals, are not representative of the original mikkyo of the ninja's ancestors. As ninja today, we are not interested in or associated with any religion. However, the original universal principles of causation, power, and enlightenment, which later became watered down to result in the countless religions of mankind, are of great interest to us.

The practice of power generation through mikkyo involves the combined use of *mantra* (sacred or "charged" words), *mandala* (schematic pictorial renderings of the structure of the universe, for the directing of concentration), and *mudra* (energy-channeling hand posturings) for the total coordination of all the energies of the personality. Bringing together thought, word, and deed in harmonious alignment where each quality complements the other is seen to be the key to working one's will in the world. This power is referred to as the *sanmitsu,* or three secrets of mikkyo spiritual power.

Japanese word	Sanskrit concept	English equivalent	Symbolizes:	*Sanmitsu*
Nenriki	mandala	concentrated intention	the will	thought
Jumon	mantra	power words	the intellect	word
Ketsu-in	mudra	hand posturings	physical action	deed

Nin-po mikkyo, the ninja's spiritual power teaching, provides two distinctive views of the structure of the universe, each view depicted in a highly symbolic diagram known as a mandala. The two mandalas represent totally opposite perspectives and are used in conjunction with each other to inspire the insight necessary to capture the significance of why the universe operates the way it does. In greatly oversimplified terms, the universal process can be viewed from the inside out, concentrating on the physical manifestations of creation and working toward an understanding of the universal laws (effect explains the cause), or the universe can be regarded from a viewpoint of total scope, concentrating on gaining a knowledge of the universal laws and working toward an understanding of the intricate interworkings of all aspects of daily life (cause explains the effect).

The essence of the material world is captured in the *taizokai* mandala, the schematic rendering of the "matrix realm." Matrix is used here in its original concept of "womb," or place in which something originates. From this approach, we come to realize that we all exist *within* the universe. Each star, planet, human, animal, thing, word, thought—indeed everything on which a label could be hung—is a part of all the parts that interact to make up what we know as the universe. All of us and all our actions are seen and acknowledged as existing within the inside of the god, just as the god is conversely seen to exist within each of us. As a means of approaching enlightenment, the taizokai mandala structure and symbols are studied for the clues necessary to bring about a realization of the universal laws that are manifested in the ways that daily worldly life unfolds. Through personal experience of our individual consciousness operating at different levels, the greater perspectives inherent in the lessons of life are brought into focus. We can come to see that the universe is vast enough and complex enough to contain all the contradiction and paradox that mankind's limited vision seems to observe.

The essence of the spiritual world is likewise captured in the *kongokai* mandala, a schematic rendering of the diamond realm. The diamond is considered to be the symbol of multi-faceted clarity, brillliance, and hardness; the jewel that is the highest possible refinement of form for unmanifested pure knowledge, spirit, or ultimate truth. From the kongokai approach, we come to realize that all in existence is merely the form that our awareness gives to the universal laws in operation around us. What we would see as or believe to be "reality" is our subjective realization of "actuality," or that which is in action itself or that which acts in its purest form. By transcending and leaving behind the material world through the mystic's process and going directly to the experience of the universal law itself, we can attain the state of *shin-shin shin-gan,* or "the mind and eyes of god," from which we can look back into the material world with a heightened, enlightened perspective.

In the nin-po mikkyo dojo, or "training hall for the learning of the ninja's secret knowledge," the mandala symbolic representations are hung on both sides of the open hall. From the viewpoint of the position of power in the dojo (the central point of focus opposite the entrance) the kongokai mandala is on the right and the taizokai mandala is on the left. These positions would, of course, be just the reverse for students in the dojo, who

WEST

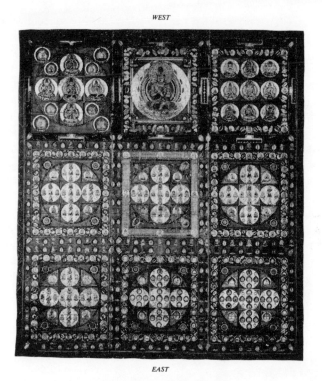

EAST

The Kongokai Mandala

face the central point of focus rather than look out from it. The mandalas are hung vertically, although their true concept is mentally laid out on a horizontal plane, creating the effect felt when looking at a city map tacked up on a wall.

When considering one of the two mandalas in meditation, the practitioner can study each particular mandala in light of the purpose of the unique piece of artwork. When contemplating the taizokai mandala of the matrix realm, the ninja looks within him or herself for an understanding of the material world. It is a falling inward process of going to the center of our very being and thereby reaching the center of the universe. When contemplating the kongokai mandala of the diamond realm, the ninja transcends him or herself for an understanding of the world of universal laws. This is a lifting outward process of leaving the self behind to attain a cosmic vision of totality. The two practices must complement each other for balanced personal development.

Undue emphasis on either of the two realms will produce a warped personality. Those who would concentrate exclusively on the material realm will become overly mechanical and technical in their outlooks, and their ninja art will become nothing more than a mere mechanistic system of physical combat, devoid of morality, spirit, and life. Those who would concentrate exclusively on the realm of pure knowledge will lose touch with reality around them, and their ninja art will become nothing more than an empty ideal or intellectual exercise, devoid of practicality, relevance, and energy.

Words and actions are useless without the guidance of thought behind them. Direction is necessary. The power of concentrated intention is a subtle lesson picked up through determined perseverence in coming to a personal understanding of the significance of the two mandalas. This is the first step, and is referred to as tempering the will.

The power of the will is then more firmly established through spoken vows that plant the intentions firmly in the realm of the physical by giving them the reality of vibratory presence. The ninja's thoughts are creations that become real "things" once they have been given physical sounds to carry them out into the world.

Chinese Lion-Dogs

Stone Chinese lion-dogs guard the temple entrance and greet initiates with a roaring "ahh-ohh-mumm-nnn" *jumon* vow, the mantra of the totality of the universe. The animal in the foreground represents the matrix realm, the material world, the left side of universal power, and the *in* side of the *in-yo* polarity (taoist *yin-yang* in Chinese). His jaws are wide open with the "ahh" seed syllable of the *taizokai* mandala. The lion-dog in the background represents the diamond realm, the world of pure wisdom, the right side of universal power, and the *yo* side of the *in-yo* polarity. His jaws are clamped shut with the "vmm" seed syllable characteristic of the kongokai mandala. Together, the two animals are a symbol of the indivisibility of the two realms that simultaneously occupy the identical time and space in the universe.

The Kane

In the ritual *kane,* the bell portion represents the *taizokai* material realm, and the *vajra* handle represents the *kongokai* realm of pure wisdom. The blending of the two in one single object symbolizes the unity existing between the physical and spiritual worlds. The ceremonial bell reminds the ninja of the truth of impermanence, a concept integral to nin-po mikkyo. The phenomenal world is like the sound that the *kane* bell emits; it can be perceived but cannot be kept. Like the sound of the bell, all things are transitory and exist only through the senses of the observer. Even life itself is like the peal of a bell, ever changing, inconstant, unstable, and predestined to the impermanence which is the essence of all things. For the ninja, realizing the significance of this impermanence is one key to approaching enlightenment.

The Kongo, and the Taizokai

The mikkyo *kongo,* or Tibetan diamond thunderbolt, symbol of the *kongokai* diamond realm. The indestructible hardness and clarity of the diamond symbolizes the power of truth and illumination to smash through ignorance and illusion. The three points represent the ability of thought, word, and deed to produce enlightenment. Meditation on the *kongokai* right hand of the universe concerns itself with the question, "What is the actual ultimate truth?" Symbolic of the finite material world, the rosary of 27 skulls depicts the *taizokai* matrix realm. The nine levels of power as realized through the three working methods of the physical, intellectual, and spiritual make up this symbol of the left hand of the universe. Meditation on the *taizokai* concept concerns itself with the question, "How can ultimate truth be realized?"

The doctrine of tantra, which teaches methods of using the powers of the physical world to bring about personal enlightenment, asserts that the process of producing sound epitomizes the evergoing process of creating the universe. The first tangible manifestations of the absolute were made in the form of sounds, or vibrations. The tantric teachings of nin-po mikkyo preserve the symbols of these fundamental vibratory rates in *shuji,* or "seed" characters, the written form of Sanskrit used between the fourth and sixth centuries during the Gupta Dynasty in India. This *siddham* script was introduced into China for the writing of tantric formulas by the Indian patriarchs teaching there, and was later carried to Japan by the monk Kukai in the ninth century. The writing form has since been preserved by the esoteric tradition in Japan, of which the ninja played a major part in the 12th through 16th centuries.

The *jumon* mantras, or "charged words of power," of the ninja's mikkyo are sounds or phrases used to give vibratory reality to the intentions of the ninja. In most instances, the jumon vows are uttered in the original language transmitted from the Himalayas, although some of the vows are voiced in classical Japanese. The jumon are intentionally preserved in words that have no meaning in daily routine conversation so that the ninja can express his or her pure determination through sound forms that can not be watered down or lessened in intensity by reflecting daily social interaction. The sounds imply interaction on a level much higher than a conversation between two intellects. The original sounds are also thought to be purer, or closer to the specific rates of vibration that will harmonize with and bear effect on the other vibrations that constitute physical reality—sights, sounds, feelings, and so forth.

Since it is the actual resonant sound itself and not the literal meaning of the words that makes the jumon effective, no attempt can be made in this volume to give instruction in the use of the voiced mantras. It could also be argued that the entire esoteric formula of how to set the mind, tune the vibrations of the voice, and engage the body should not appear in specific notation in a published volume such as this. Those individuals who feel it their destiny to become a part of the ninja tradition will seek out the teacher that they need for such advanced training in the total power of ninjutsu.

For the purposes of information only, it is possible to grasp a small experience of the nin-po mikkyo jumon through the vocalization of two primary sounds, one blending into the other. Open your mouth and throat as wide as you can, creating the sensation of a yawn. Tightening your stomach slowly, breathe out through your mouth while producing a full-throated sighing sound from deep within your body. It should sound like a breathy, resonant "ahh." Continue the sound and bring your lips together, stretching them over your parted teeth to close your mouth while maintaining your jaws in open position. The tone should now be a buzzing, vibrant "mmm." Continue the original sound and bring your teeth together firmly, compacting your tongue against the inside surfaces of your clenched teeth. The tone should now be a level, vibrating "nnn." Allow the sound to die away slowly as you expel the last of your breath.

This series of sound groupings blended into one continuous "word" is considered to be the ultimate universal mantra. The majority of the ninja jumon vows begin with this sound, much in the fashion of the universal "ahh-menn" that ends the hymns and chants of the Christian faith. When voiced repeatedly in syncronization with a large group of other people in a cool, darkened room (to reduce sensual distractions), the "ahh-ohh-mmm-nnn" mantra blends the personal breathing rhythms, voice qualities, and spiritual intensities of each individual. When practiced with people who are thoroughly enjoying themselves while not taking themselves overly seriously, the resultant effect can be quite awesome.

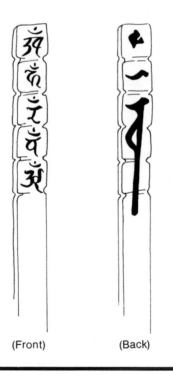

(Front) (Back)

Shuji

Shuji written characters, visual symbols of the power of the various levels of vibratory energy, inscribed on the walking staffs of *yamabushi* mountain warrior priests. The five characters (sounds) ["ah, vah, rah, hah, khah"] on one side represent the earth, water, fire, wind, and void of the matrix realm material world. The single seed sound ("vahmm") on the opposite side is the symbol of the pure knowledge of the diamond realm. The construction of the staff attests to the ninja's belief that the two realms are mere reflections of each other.

The third area of knowledge required for mastery of nin-po mikkyo's *sanmitsu* three secrets of power is the body's incorporation in the task of creating a reality from the intention formulated by the will and expressed through the voice as a vow. The *kuji-in* finger entwining hand "seals" of ninjutsu stem from the mudra hand postures of Indian, Tibetan, and Chinese esoteric lore, and represent the channeling of subtle energies, the transmitting of lessons in wisdom, and the affording of psychic protection to self and others.

In the electrochemical makeup of the human body, a collection of electropolar channels (meridians) run through the tissues of the body. The hands and feet are thought to contain the sensitive ends and turn-around points of the channels. Ninjutsu's *kuji-in* (nine-syllable mudras) and their

Left Hand	Right Hand
Taizokai (material world)	*Kongokai* (pure wisdom)
Moon	Sun
Temporal reality	Ultimate actuality
Inner	Outer
Worldly beings	Gods
Healing	Power
In	*Yo*
Arresting the active mind	Realization of pure knowledge
Receiving	Projecting
Negative (–)	Positive (+)

Little Finger	Ring Finger	Middle Finger	Pointer	Thumb
Earth	Water	Fire	Wind	Void
Physical body	Emotions	Intellect	Wisdom	Communication
Rocks	Plants	Animals	Mankind	Sub-atomic particles
Stability	Adaptability	Aggression	Benevolence	Creativity
Chi	*Sui*	*Ka*	*Fu*	*Ku*
地	水	火	風	空

variations comprise a power generating system based on a balancing out or directing of energy through the hands. In this system, each hand and finger symbolize a specific attribute of the body's makeup. Different energies of the personality are represented by element and structure codes. Concentration and stress on the various energies could result in an alternation of the body's mood, bearing, and predominant capability at any given moment.

Nin-po mikkyo's *kuji goshin ho*—nine syllable method of protection— is one of several mudra, mantra, and mandala combinations perfected by the ninja for increased sensitivity to the workings of all around him. Effected before going into action or entering a threatening place, the nine hand poses and syllables work to sharpen the ninja's senses as a means for increasing the likelihood of success. Each of the nine hand poses, when used separately, has its own unique mantra sentence and mind setting procedure, which are not included in this volume.

It should be noted that the physical examples of the hand positions that follow are provided as illustrations only. They are by no means complete lessons in themselves. Merely folding the fingers and making a sound with the voice will not produce any recognizable effect on the personality. Anyone wishing to develop a control over the subtle energies of the body must devote a considerable amount of study and concentration to build up skill in the *kuji-in* process. The crucial mind setting and breathing routines have not been included here, as they must be guided personally by a competent teacher of ninjutsu. This series of hand positions and vows is presented here for its information value only.

"Rin, pyo, toh, sha, kai, jin, rets', sai, zen," is the jumon vow that accompanies the weaving of the fingers for each of the nine steps, or "levels of power." Each of the syllables has its own hand pose, which in turn has its own jumon chant or vow that calls upon a particular personification of some cosmic aspect or diety for assistance in directing power. In effect, the ninja selects a goal of emulation and then becomes that goal in thought, word, and deed, by attuning his or her body, voice, and mental imagery with the desired outcome. The entire personality then takes on the feel that the goal has already been accomplished, and is merely awaiting the proper time to physically manifest itself.

Rin
Dokko-in (sign of the *vajra* Tibetan thunderbolt)

The physical imitation of the mikkyo *dokko* or *kongo* "diamond thunderbolt" which represents the awesome power of wisdom and pure knowledge as it smashes through crudeness and ignorance, the dokko-in is used to inspire the strength for overcoming physical and mental trials, and for prevailing over all that would crush the ninja.

Pyo
Daikongo-in (sign of the great diamond)

The physical imitation of the diamond, symbol of the power of knowledge which transcends the worldly limitations, the daikongo-in is used to inspire personal power through the channeling of energy to the appropriate area of consciousness for the purpose at hand.

Toh
Sotojishi-in (sign of the outer lion)

The lion has merely to roar, and all other animals surrender to him. This hand tying signifies the successful surrendering to the lion outside of us, or attaining what we need while going along with whatever confronts us. By coming into attunement with the forces of fate, the ninja can develop the *ki-ai* to foresee and go along with the scheme of totality. The sotojishi-in is used to inspire the insight for traveling with the process of the universe.

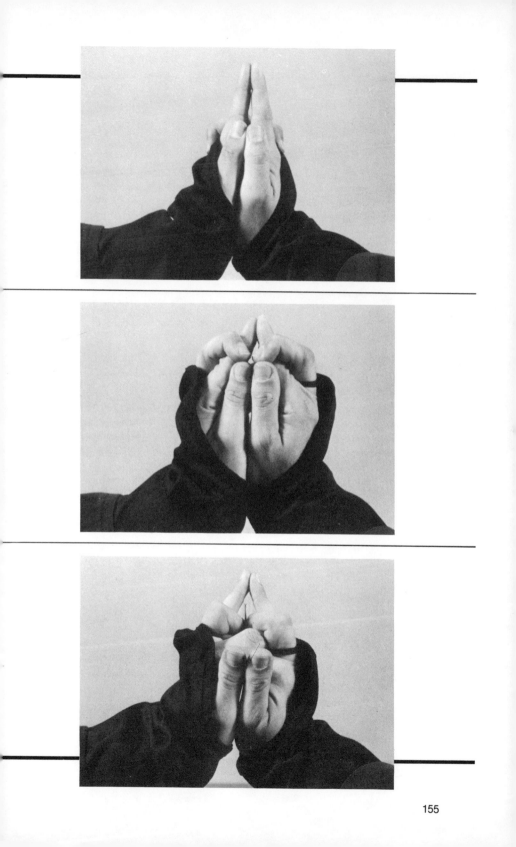

Sha
Uchijishi-in (sign of the inner lion)

The internal workings of our bodies are symbolized by the lion within. Our health can provide us with enormous power or can destroy all chances for accomplishment in this lifetime. The uchijishi-in, along with the proper jumon vow, is used to generate the energy for healing self and others, and to promote healthy surroundings.

Kai
Gebakuken-in (sign of the outer bonds fist)

The passions that bind us to illusions prevent us from receiving all that our consciousness is capable of taking in. The gebakuken-in represents the ninja working toward the attributes of the god by letting go of the bonds, and is used to inspire an expanded awareness that will allow the ninja to feel the approach of a premonition of danger.

Jin
Naibakuken-in (sign of the inner bonds fist)

The mind's insistence on limiting its intake to physical sense data must be overcome before the ninja can employ the full powers of enlightenment. The naibakuken-in represents the ninja relying on the cosmic consciousness of the god by accepting the reality of intuition, and is used to attune the awareness towards knowing the thoughts of others and projecting thoughts to others.

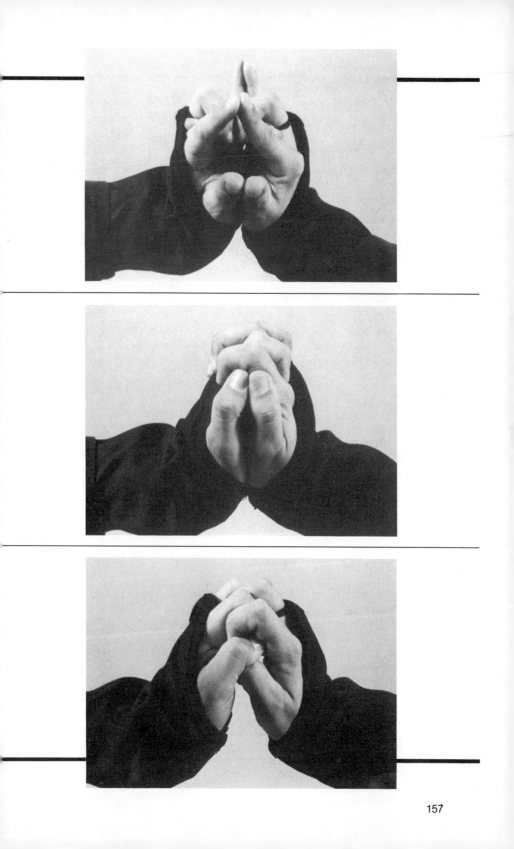

Retsu
Chiken-in (sign of the wisdom fist)

Mankind in the material world, represented by the upraised left index finger, is totally surrounded by the power and protection of the actuality of pure knowledge, represented by the right hand. The two hands together represent the oneness of the taizokai material realm and the kongokai spiritual realm, and the oneness of the individual soul and cosmic soul. The chiken-in figuratively frees the ninja from the limits of time and space, and is used to assist the ninja in focusing on distant places and other times as sources of knowledge for application in the present time and place.

Zai
Nichirin-in (sign of the ring of the sun)

The body of flame is triangular, and the triangle symbolizes the fire which must destroy all that is impure and stands in the way of *sammaji,* or the elevating of the mind beyond material reality to a plane where it is one with the unity of the universe. The nichirin-in is used to transport the ninja to a point of oneness with the source of all manifestation in the universe, where directions and physical forms of matter can be altered and controlled through the power of the will alone.

Zen
Ongyo-in (sign of the concealed form)

The ninja's power and perspective in life comes from an enlightenment that can be resented and scoffed at by lesser souls lacking enlightenment. Therefore a part of that enlightenment is a knowledge of the ways to become invisible. Along with the proper jumon recitation and mind set, the ongyo-in is used to obtain the protection of cosmic forces in order to become invisible to all lowly, resentful, and evil people, and to vanish in the face of disaster.

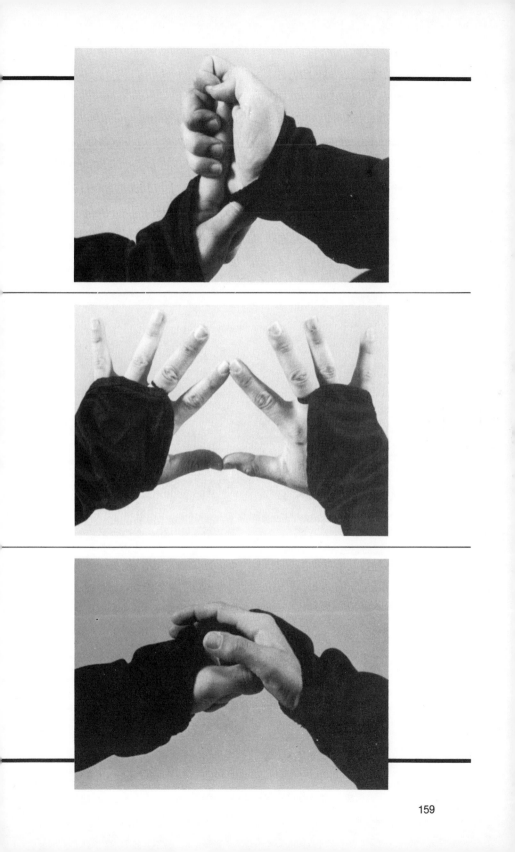